HOME *sweet* HOME

THE LITTLE BOOK OF NATURAL CLEANING

sphere

First published in Great Britain in 2020 by Sphere

10 9 8 7 6 5 4 3 2 1

The moral right of the author has been asserted.

A CIP catalogue record for this book is available from the British Library.

ISBN 978-0-7515-8057-0

Printed and bound in in Italy by L.E.G.O. S.p.A.

Papers used by Sphere are from well-managed forests and other
responsible sources.

Sphere
An imprint of
Little, Brown Book Group
Carmelite House
50 Victoria Embankment
London EC4Y 0DZ

An Hachette UK Company
www.hachette.co.uk

www.littlebrown.co.uk

Contents

INTRODUCTION

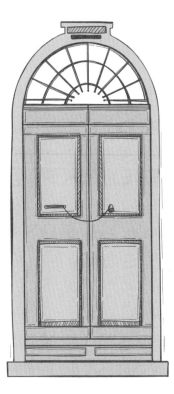

Home is where the heart is...

Home is the place where everyone should feel happy and at peace – and that means a house that is clean, safe and welcoming to all.

Using traditional, natural cleaning methods to tackle everyday chores is not only a simple and effective way to help the environment, but also helps safeguard your family, friends and pets from the potentially harmful side-effects of many modern cleaning products.

'There is nothing like
staying at home for
real comfort'

JANE AUSTEN

Six Reasons to Clean Naturally

1. *It's safer*

Making your own natural products means you can keep your home free from toxic chemicals.

2. *It's cheaper*

You only need a handful of natural ingredients to clean your entire home from top to bottom! No need to splash out on a different expensive product for every room.

3. *It's easy*

Most homemade natural cleaning products contain minimal ingredients that can be mixed quickly and easily for maximum impact!

4. *It's kinder*

   Natural cleaning products are gentler
   on your furniture and fabrics, helping to
   ensure they stay looking good for longer!

5. *It's greener*

   Making your own natural cleaning products
   reduces the amount of harmful chemicals
   entering the eco-system and cuts down on
   plastic packaging.

6. *It works!*

   Traditional cleaning methods are just as
   effective as modern products at dealing
   with dirt and stains – and they smell great!

'*People usually are the happiest at home*'

WILLIAM SHAKESPEARE

STORE CUPBOARD
ESSENTIALS

Lemons

You might think lemon is only useful for its fresh, zesty scent, but the acidic juices and the oils contained within the peel can be used in multiple ways to make your home sparkle!

When life gives you lemons . . .

❧ Lemons have antibacterial and antiseptic
  qualities.

❧ Lemon juice can be used as gentle bleach.

- Lemons don't just smell good, they are active deodorisers that can neutralise bad odours in the home.

- The essential oil (see page 45) extracted from lemon peel can be used in homemade furniture polish and to scent your other natural cleaning products.

*Easy Peasy
Lemon Squeezy*

Vinegar

'You catch more flies with honey than vinegar . . .'

But you clean more surfaces with vinegar!

For generations, this versatile and
cost-effective condiment has been used
by canny cleaners to tackle the most
stubborn household grease and stains.

Not just for your chips!

🐦 White vinegar (sometimes called distilled vinegar) is a powerful cleaning agent because it is very acidic. Always read the label carefully to see if it is safe to use in cooking.

🐦 The high acid content means white vinegar can easily cut through grease and build-ups of soap scum in your kitchen and bathroom.

꙰ Vinegar can also be used to make your windows and stainless-steel appliances shine like they're brand new!

꙰ Gentler vinegars like Cider Apple and Malt (chip shop!) vinegar also have many uses around the home.

Vinegar should always be diluted with water! See page 49 for some tips on using natural cleaning products safely around the home.

Baking Soda

This wonder product (also known as bicarbonate of soda) not only helps your cakes magically rise in the oven, but can also be used throughout the home to safely clean surfaces and tackle bad smells.

The Super-Hero Secret Ingredient!

• Baking soda is a natural abrasive that, when mixed with water, can be used to scour surfaces.

• Baking soda can be used to absorb unpleasant smells around the home – especially in the fridge.

• You can easily bulk-buy baking soda, rather than those little tubs we use for baking. Much more cost-effective!

- Baking soda can also be used throughout the laundry cycle, including as a safe and natural fabric softener.

- Be careful not to confuse Baking Soda or Bicarbonate of Soda with Baking Powder, which has additional ingredients that make it perfect for cooking but less effective for cleaning!

TOP TIP!

Never mix baking soda and vinegar – they cancel each other out, making the resulting mixture ineffective. And if stored in a sealed container, the vinegar can cause the soda to foam which could lead to a messy explosion in your cupboard!

Olive Oil

Long before we started pouring olive oil onto our salads, it was sold in pharmacies as a home remedy. Nowadays it's widely available on supermarket shelves, but also has many uses outside the kitchen.

Oil be there for you . . .

∻ Olive oil can be used to nourish and
protect wooden surfaces, such as kitchen
countertops or dining-room tables.

∻ It can also be used to bring your stainless-
steel appliances to a high shine and to
prevent tarnishing on silverware.

- Leather sofas and chairs also love a bit of olive oil – a gentle application can help keep leather supple and improve the appearance of any scratches.

- When mixed with an abrasive like salt, olive oil can be used to scour cast iron pans.

Salt

ε• Rock salt or everyday table salt are both
  natural abrasives than can be combined
  with other ingredients to create pastes that
  will help shift all sorts of stubborn marks.

ε• Salt can also be used immediately on
  red-wine, grease and ink spills to prevent
  staining – simply blot away the excess liquid
  and then leave the salt absorb the stain
  over time. Then vacuum away!

STORE CUPBOARD
EXTRAS

With the five simple natural ingredients listed in the last chapter, you'll be able to clean your whole house from top to bottom. But to give your cleaning routine a bit of extra help, you might want to keep these additional items on hand . . .

- **Empty spray bottles** – thoroughly clean old bottles to use for your new, natural cleaning products.

- **Soda crystals** – useful for tackling stubborn limescale and unclogging blocked sinks.

- **Distilled water** – can be useful for some recipes and is easily available online.

- **Castile soap** – this entirely natural, traditionally made soap can be used throughout the home, and as a natural body wash or shampoo.

- **Rubbing alcohol** – handy for cleaning wounds and around the house!

- **A selection of recycled, reusable cleaning cloths** – by repurposing old towels, sheets and T-shirts, you will save money and reduce the amount of waste going to landfill.

- **Traditional wooden dish brushes** (many with replaceable heads) are now widely available online, as are plastic-free sponges.

- **Vodka** – and not just for a post-cleaning cocktail! This strong alcohol performs many of the same functions as vinegar but has the benefit of being completely odour free.

'Love begins at home'

MOTHER THERESA

ESSENTIAL

OILS

Essential oils are made from the highly concentrated extracts of plants and are used widely in traditional medicine and throughout the home. In addition to their beautiful and therapeutic aromas, they are thought to have many health benefits and anti-microbial properties that can safeguard your home from nasty germs.

Essential oils should never be taken internally and can be harmful if used undiluted on the skin. Always read the instructions very carefully before using.

Essential Essential Oils for Cleaning!

1. **Tea Tree Oil** – known for its antiseptic
   and anti-microbial properties, Tea Tree oil
   can be used in a natural all-purpose cleaner
   and as an air purifier.

2. **Lemon Oil** – acts as a more potent version
   of lemon juice, with powerful de-greasing
   abilities and a lovely, fresh scent. It can also
   be used in furniture polishes.

3. **Lavender Oil** – lavender is famous for its calming aroma and is a popular scent around the home. It can also be used in laundry and to freshen up linens.

4. **Cinnamon Oil** – this strongly scented oil can be used to fight mould . . . and will make your house smell like Christmas!

Safety Tips

Although none of these natural ingredients are inherently harmful, you should always be sensible when mixing together powerful ingredients and cautious about getting any mixtures on your skin or in your eye.

- Never ingest essential oils or use undiluted on the skin.

- Check the label of any vinegar product you buy in the cleaning aisle if you intend to use it for any other purpose – it may not be safe for consumption.

- Always clearly label any mixture you intend to store for the long term.

- Don't mix vinegar and baking soda!

- Undiluted vinegar can damage surfaces – always mix with water.

- Test any homemade product on a small and discreet patch before using.

- To ensure you are eliminating dangerous bacteria such as E. coli and salmonella, use white vinegar in your homemade surface spray.

HOW
NATURAL
CLEANING
CAN PROTECT
THE PLANET

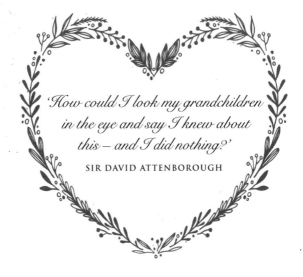

'How could I look my grandchildren in the eye and say I knew about this – and I did nothing?'

SIR DAVID ATTENBOROUGH

Many household cleaners contain powerful ingredients that are causing lasting damage to the planet. These toxic chemicals pollute our waterways and land, entering the food chain and even ending up in our own drinking water.

It is also thought that some of these chemicals could have lasting effects on our health.

'It is our collective and individual
responsibility to preserve and
tend to the world in which
we all live'

DALAI LAMA

Eight million tonnes of plastic end up in the ocean each year, killing marine life and depositing harmful mircoplastics into the food chain.

Reducing our consumption of single-use plastic items (such as straws, water bottles and coffee cups) and being more mindful about how we dispose of plastic items can have an enormous impact on the wellbeing of the planet.

Disposable wipes (such as baby wipes, cleaning wipes and face cleansing wipes) are responsible for blocking sewers, damaging our rivers and polluting the oceans with the microplastics they contain.

The Marine Conservation Society found over 27 wipes per 100 metres of the UK coastline in 2017, an increase of 94% on the previous year. Never dispose of a wipe down the toilet, even if it claims to be flushable!

Why not try making your own reusable wipes instead?

In a large air-tight jar, mix 175 ml of distilled water (or alternatively use boiled and cooled filtered water), 25 ml of white vinegar, half a teaspoon of Castile soap and 30 drops of your favourite essential oil. Gently stir and stuff jar with squares of clean fabric (squares of an old T-shirt work well) and then seal.

Voila! Your own easy-to-use, cheap and ocean-friendly wipes!

'No one is too small to
make a difference'

GRETA THUNBERG

THE
UNEXPECTED
BENEFITS OF
CLEANING

෴ Clean homes – and especially clean
   kitchens – dramatically reduce the
   possibility of illness transmitted by bacteria
   such as E. coli and Salmonella.

෴ Cluttered and untidy homes have been
   found to lead to increased levels of the
   stress hormone cortisol. So, it's true what
   they say: *tidy home, tidy mind*.

- Household chores can keep you fit! It's been estimated that vacuuming burns 100 calories every hour.

- Allergies are reduced in a house with less dust and pet hairs.

- And best of all, you're always ready to welcome friends and family into a home you can be proud of.

THE KITCHEN

Natural Surface Cleaner

ও The essential ingredients for a natural anti-bacterial spray for surfaces where food is being prepared or eaten are water and white vinegar.

ও Vinegar should always be diluted with water, usually in a 1:1 ratio. *Warning: do not use vinegar sprays on granite, marble or other natural stone floors or surfaces.*

꒰ The vinegary smell will disappear quickly, but if you want to fragrance your spray, try infusing the vinegar with lemons. Simply pour the vinegar over lemon segments (they can be previously squeezed!) and keep in an air-tight jar for two weeks before mixing your spray.

꒰ Alternatively, you can add your favourite essential oils – simply drop into the water and vinegar mixture and then shake to distribute.

Fridge deodoriser

❧ Simply keeping an open container of baking soda in the fridge can help eliminate unpleasant odours.

❧ Try placing slices of lemon, sprinkled in salt and baking soda, on a saucer in the fridge – this will help absorb any bad smells and freshen up the fridge with a lemon-fresh scent.

'Home is the nicest word
there is'

LAURA INGALLS WILDER

Oven cleaner

A paste of baking soda (three tablespoons) and water (1.5 tablespoons) applied to your oven door and interior – avoiding the heating element – and left for a minimum of twenty minutes should help to shift even the most stubborn grime. Then just wipe away with a clean cloth.

Washing-Up Liquid

A 1:1 ratio of Castile soap to water makes an effective alternative to washing-up liquid. It won't foam as much as the brands you're used to, but that doesn't mean it's not working.

Adding baking soda will help add an abrasive element to the mixture that can help to shift stubborn grime. As ever, essential oils can add a nice scent to make doing the dishes more pleasant!

Kettle De-scaler

A 1:1 ratio of white vinegar to water will
help remove limescale from your kettle.
Leave the mixture in the kettle for at least
one hour, then pour away the liquid and
wipe away any of the dislodged scum.
Rinse your kettle thoroughly before making
your next cup of tea!

Floor Cleaner

This all-purpose floor cleaner can be used on your kitchen floor to wipe away every-day grime. You need . . .

* 250 ml of white vinegar
* 250 ml of rubbing alcohol, which will help your floors dry more quickly
* 4 litres of hot water
* Essential oils for scent

Mix together in a large bucket and you're all set!

'The ache for home
lives in all of us'

MAYA ANGELOU

Drain Unblocker

To clear a blocked sink, simply pour a mug of soda crystals down the drain and then follow with a kettle of hot water. If that doesn't do the trick, then you can try soda crystals with a splash of white vinegar – the chemical reaction should shift any build up.

LAUNDRY

'Family is a life jacket
in the stormy sea of life'

J.K. ROWLING

Laundry has one of the biggest and most harmful effects on the environment. Aside from the damaging impact of detergents polluting our waterways, washing machines also use an enormous amount of water and electricity. But simple steps can have a massive impact.

If you go anywhere,
even paradise, you will
miss your home'

MALALA YOUSAFZAI

Green Laundry Tips

- Washing your clothes at 30 °C helps to reduce the amount of electricity your washing machine uses.

- Consider drying your clothes the old-fashioned way – on an airer or the washing-line – rather than using a tumble drier.

- Switch to eco-friendly brands of detergent and fabric conditioner. Or, better yet, make your own . . .

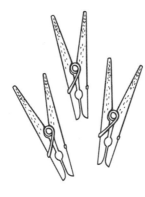

Laundry detergent

A safe, natural homemade laundry detergent needs only two ingredients:

* 500 ml washing soda
* A bar of Castile soap

To scent your mixture (and for added stain-removing power) you can add lemon essential oil. Try adding a spoonful of baking soda to deal with unpleasant odours.

Grate your bar of Castile soap and add to your washing soda and mix well. Use one to two tablespoons per load. If desired, add a few drops of essential oils to the drum.

How to Make Washing Soda

You can buy washing soda ready-made, but
did you know that if you *bake* baking soda,
it turns into washing soda? Simply pour
a thick layer (approximately 1.5 cm) of
baking soda into the base of an ovenproof
dish and cook at 200 °C for half an hour
or until it has changed from a light, dusty
consistency into a more granular texture.
Cool and store in an airtight jar.

Fabric Softener

This simple mixture will make your family's clothes super soft – the natural way!

* 1.5 litres of white vinegar
* 350 grams baking soda
* 15 drops essential oil (optional)

Pour the vinegar into a large bowl and add your essential oil. Then add your baking soda. When the fizzing stops, pour into an airtight container. Use up to 1 cup per load.

'The objective of cleaning is not just to clean, but to feel happiness living within that environment'

MARIE KONDO

Tough Stains

These natural ingredients can be used to help shift stubborn stains on your clothes

- **White vinegar** – boost your laundry cycle by adding a cup of vinegar to the wash.

- **Baking soda** – makes your whites whiter if you add to the wash and is a natural deodoriser.

- **Lemon** – use as a gentle bleach to return whites to their former glory. Simply apply to the fabric and lay out in the sun.

Lavender Bags

A small bag of lavender tucked in among your clothes will not only keep things smelling fresh but can also act as a natural moth repellent.

These little sachets are easy to make and last for ages!

* Prepare a mixture of dried lavender flowers and dry rice.

* Cut two squares of fabric – approximately 10 cm x 10 cm.

* Sew three sides of the squares together to make a bag. Sewing the bag inside out and then reversing will make a neater finish.

* Fill the bag with the lavender and rice mixture.

* Either sew up the fourth side or tie securely together with a piece of ribbon.

THE
BATHROOM

Bathroom Spray

The surface spray on page 66 will work equally well in your bathroom to clean your sink, bath and shower, but why not add germ-killing Tea Tree oil to your vinegar and water mixture for a bit of added oomph?

If your bathroom requires something more powerful, read on!

Toilet Cleaner

Can you clean the loo without bleach?
Yes! It can easily be done with this simple
recipe .

* 240 ml white vinegar
* ½ teaspoon Tea Tree oil

Spray the vinegar and essential oil mixture
around the bowl and on the seat, lid
and handle. Leave for several minutes.
Meanwhile, sprinkle baking soda inside
the bowl and scrub with a toilet brush. Use
a clean dry cloth to remove the vinegar
solution.

'I think that when you invite people to your home, you invite them to yourself'

OPRAH WINFREY

Tile Scrub

Sometimes our bathroom tiles need a
good old scrub with something abrasive to
remove a build-up of soap and grime.

Spray the tiles with a vinegar solution
(see page 66) and then scour with a sponge
and baking soda to remove any build-up.
Rinse with water and reveal your sparkling
clean tiles!

Air Freshener

This can be used throughout the house but is particularly useful in the bathroom!

Simply mix 175 ml of water with two tablespoons of rubbing alcohol or vodka and several drops of the essential oil of your choice in a small spray bottle. Shake and spray!

The Power of Scent

Try using these essential oils throughout the house to create a different mood in every room . . .

🖎 Lavender in the bedroom to help relaxation before sleep.

🖎 Lemon in the kitchen for a fresh, clean smell to awaken the senses.

- Vanilla in the living room for a warm, welcoming atmosphere to unwind in.

- Tea Tree in the bathroom for a wake-me-up scent first thing in the morning.

LIVING ROOM

Glass and Window Cleaner

The traditional method for cleaning
windows is still used by many people
today as it can't be beaten! Vinegar and
newspaper applied to dirty windows and
mirrors is a sure-fire way to ensure a streak-
free, sparkling finish.

* Mix a solution of one part white vinegar to one part water in a spray bottle.
* Spray onto window or mirror.
* Wipe dry with newspaper to achieve a streak-free finish.

If your window is very grimy, try washing with soapy water first to remove the worst of the dirt, then follow with the vinegar solution.

Furniture Polish

This simple recipe will nourish and restore your wooden furniture.

* 2 parts olive oil
* 2 parts white vinegar
* 1 part lemon juice
* Mix all ingredients and use a cloth to apply to your wooden furniture.

'Home is where one
starts from'

T. S. ELIOT

Carpet Stain Remover

When you spot a stain on your carpet
or rug, the first thing to do is absorb as
much of the liquid as possible with a cloth.
Never rub it in! If the stain has already
dried, try brushing or vacuuming off any
excess before tackling the underlying stain.
Different stains react to different cleaning
solutions, but the following recipe is good
all-rounder on most day-to-day spills.

* 250 ml white vinegar

* 500 ml water

* 2 tsp salt

* 15 drops essential oil

Simply add all the ingredients into a spray bottle, shake and then spray onto the stained area. Leave to dry and then vacuum.

Fabric Refresher

Sometimes the upholstery in our homes
needs a little help to stay fresh. Rather
than dousing in chemicals that can damage
expensive fabrics, this homemade natural
spray will tackle lingering odours and leave
your sofas smelling good as new.

Fill a small spray bottle with heated
distilled water and add one tablespoon
of baking soda, which will dissolve in
the warm liquid. Add ten drops of your
favourite essential oil and spray directly
onto the fabric.

'Many people will walk in and out of your life, but only true friends will leave footprints in your heart'

ELEANOR ROOSEVELT

TOP TIP!

Don't forget to patch test any homemade mixture before using! Try spraying this upholstery refresher on a small section of fabric that won't be noticeable in the unlikely event that there is any adverse effect.

FURRY FRIENDS

'Dogs are better than
human beings because they
know but do not tell'

EMILY DICKINSON

Pets Love Natural Cleaning Too!

Toxic chemicals in the home can be harmful to our cats, dogs and other furry friends, so cleaning naturally is safer for them too.

But as much as we love them, they do like to make a mess . . .

- If your pet has an accident on the rug, use the spray on page 116 on the stain after blotting away any excess liquid. When you've scrubbed away the worst of it, sprinkle with baking soda to lift the remaining smell. When dry, vacuum away.

- Add 100 ml of white vinegar to your wash cycle (using the laundry detergent on page 87) to help clean a stinky dog bed.

- ❧ Running your hand over any surface covered in pet hair while wearing an old rubber glove will help collect hair and make it easy to lift off.

- ❧ A very light coating of olive oil on your pet's food bowl will make it easier to clean and the oil is also good for their coats!

- ❧ A mixture of water and eucalyptus essential oil sprayed onto carpets and upholstery can help keep fleas at bay.

'What greater gift than
the love of a cat?'

CHARLES DICKENS

Bath time!

Some dogs love bath time, some hate it.
But washing their coats with a homemade,
natural shampoo means that even if
they make a fuss, you know you're using
something safe and effective on their coat
and skin. Mix together the following for
shampooing success . . .

* 125 ml of liquid Castile soap
* 75 ml of white vinegar
* 1 tablespoon of olive oil
* 3 or 4 drops of essential oil

Wet your dog with warm water and then lather in the shampoo all over. Take care to avoid the eyes, as the mixture will sting. When you're done, rinse away all the shampoo and then stand well back . . . !

Groom as usual.

'We shape our dwellings,
and afterwards our dwellings
shape us'

SIR WINSTON CHURCHILL

A safe and happy home is something we all cherish. Using natural, homemade cleaning products will protect your family, friends, pets and most beloved possessions – and help to ensure the planet is safe for generations to come.

INDEX

IMAGE CREDITS